Selected Poems
2000-2020

Winner of The Birdy Poetry Prize—2020
by Meadowlark Press

Selected Poems 2000-2020
JC Mehta

Curated & Edited by Brenna Crotty

Meadowlark Press, LLC
Emporia, Kansas USA

Meadowlark Press, LLC
meadowlark-books.com
P.O. Box 333, Emporia, KS 66801

Selected Poems: 2000-2020
Copyright ©JC Mehta, 2020

All rights reserved. This book or any portion thereof may not be reproduced or used in any manner whatsoever without the express written permission of the author except for the use of brief quotations in a book review.

Cover Design by Evie Simmons.

ISBN: 978-1-7342477-5-6

Library of Congress Control Number: 2020952622

For Maa, Nayana Mehta

Selected Poems

Editor's Notes   *1*
Place Settings   *2*
Rezervations   *3*
You Look Something   *4*
What the Body Remembers   *5*
A Catholic Funeral   *6*
An Event Worth Celebrating   *7*
Birthdays   *8*
Childhood   *9*
Disarming   *10*
Lattes and Labiaplasty   *11*
An Anorexia Thing   *12*
What the Good Lord Planted   *13*
"Passing"   *14*
Red Delicious   *15*
Nvda Diniyoli (Children of the Sun)   *16*
Recipe for Moong Daal   *17*
Alpha to Omega   *18*
Ingredients of Love   *19*
My Body, My Self   *20*
Look at All the Beautiful   *21*
Land Lords   *22*
Recipe for an Indian   *23*
Bad Indian   *24*
On the Runway   *25*
Writing   *26*
A Consenting Platypus   *27*
Pulitzer Prize Pig   *28*
Recollections of the Training Days   *29*
The Penthouse in the Pearl   *30*
The Temporary Nature of Being   *31*
~~mURDERED & mISSING iNDIGENOUS wOMEN~~*   *32*
Untitled   *34*
My Mother('s) Remains   *35*

Beebe Farms: Closed August, 2017   *36*
A Priest and an Indian Walk Into a Bar   *37*
The Lecture   *38*
To Grin Macabre   *39*
The Photograph   *40*
How to Oil an Indian Man's Hair   *41*
Let Me Go Quietly   *42*
"Eating Like a Bird, it's Really a Falsity"   *43*
Recovery   *44*
How to Talk to the Dying   *45*
Mourning Lights   *46*
All the Ways   *47*
Mark's Tumor (When I Needed it Most)   *48*
Something Beautiful   *49*
When to Stay   *50*

Acknowledgments   *51*
About the Author   *53*

Introduction

JC Mehta will tell you exactly who they are.

In 2018, while working on a collaboration between *CALYX Journal* and *Cordella Magazine*, I was lucky enough to get to reprint one of Mehta's poems, "Recipe for an Indian." The very first line demanded *How much Indian are you?* and in the same line retorted *All of it.* The poem itself—short and vivid—braided together an identity built on hunger, desirability, trauma, family, and yearning. I knew absolutely nothing about JC Mehta as a person, but I suddenly felt like I had a very clear window into who they were in only nine lines.

So when Mehta reached out and asked me to curate this collection from twenty years of their work, I had to say yes. Their poetry invited me into experiences both similar and wildly different from my own with humor and a complete lack of self-consciousness. With sharp and incisive language, each piece provides an immersive moment, inviting the reader into the experience of growing up half Cherokee, of self-harm and losing friends, of teaching and aging and loving and living in the Pacific Northwest. Nothing is veiled, nothing is alluded to, and their humor is ever-present, wry and witty. Any writer who begins a poem with *My psychologist says (don't you love when poets start like this?)* has levels of self-awareness and genre savvy that speak to years of dedication to identity and craft.

I have a great admiration for Mehta's style of poetry because I have always had a soft spot for writing that is unafraid. Occasionally brash and belligerent, occasionally tired and defeated, every poem is refreshingly honest in its self-reflection, each one adjusting a new shard of identity, large or small, to provide a glimpse at a deep and complex life. Mehta's focus is most often on the self: one's body, bloodline, trauma, relationships, and place in the community.

In "Place Settings," the very second poem in this collection, they tell the reader: *All my family's dead so nobody's / left that knows there's an Indian / girl with a sick head / who grew up poor and sometimes / likes to fuck women gone / and snuck into this little fête.* There really isn't time for florid metaphor when laying bare the self—these poems are written with a knife, not a quill.

When I received three hundred of Mehta's poems and was tasked with selecting a third of them for this book, they were sent to me in alphabetical order. Considering many of them are deeply personal and confessional poems, I found it to be a strange and immersive way to construct an image of a life and its histories, one where childhood experiences were fresh and pertinent at any moment in time, where there was no real beginning or end to an eating disorder. In choosing the order of this collection, I tried to preserve that non-linear feeling. I didn't want to construct tidy trajectories that followed poems from childhood to adulthood, from suicide attempts to recovery, mostly because Mehta's own poetry largely dismisses such neat lines and parameters. In their poem "Recovery," they ask, *Recover is a funny word, like / what's buried that needs covering / again?* The self is a fractured and complex subject throughout the book, and my hope is that a non-linear collection such as this preserves the fraught and capricious relationships that we all have to our own changing and evolving identities.

Instead of a timeline, I focused on the twin centers of Mehta's work, the *I* and the *you*. Their depiction of themself is clear and consistent, told in bold and sometimes lonely strokes, and the introduction of the *you* changes that dynamic. The *you* is always the same unnamed figure, a lover or life partner. *I want you to be the only one to say my name like it mattered. The body of my pieces I wrote for you* ("Let Me Go Quietly"). As the fragments of the *I* create a clear and vivid picture, there is a beautiful grace in the way Mehta moves their same unsentimental but deeply loving focus to another, the way it begins to encompass a *we* beyond the *I* or *you*. There is a wild serenity that develops within that concept of *we*, creating a softness even to some of the familiar edges of grief, and that is the movement that I believe is at the center of this collection.

Perhaps a little confusingly, the poem I selected as the first of the collection is titled "Editor's Notes," and I did it because it slyly addressed the questions that I had when I first read through Mehta's body of work. *Did all this really happen, did / those people really die? Did you seriously / try to kill yourself?* They already know the questions you'll have, and they have ready responses that are all the more satisfying and invigorating for their freshness and honesty. They might tell you something about you, too.

Brenna Crotty
Editor

Selected Poems

Editor's Notes

Did all this really happen, did
those people really die? Did you seriously
try to kill yourself? I imagine

it would be real hard to pretend,
to fake it
even in writing (which some of those people
told me I'm good at). Yes,

it all happened. Maybe I mixed
up the dates, left some pieces out
like the tonsils or kidneys, parts
we're born with
that don't matter much. Of course,

they all died, the whole lot.
(Even after we promised not to. Even
when I thought he was evergreen.)
I worked the funerals in somnambulism,
skipped the celebrations of life
altogether. And yes, I suppose

I truly did try to kill myself, although
it didn't start out that way. I didn't know
there's only one end to disappearing, one
final vanishing act. I'm still not sure

who pulled me out, why my fingers
weren't strong enough to hold fast
to the dirt, my feet not fast enough
to kick away those helping hands.
My death is the real slow one,
built on flirtations with the earth,
erotic asphyxiations and breath play
along a silently decaying fulcrum.

Everybody else
was so much faster, so slippery,
so better at all this than me.

Place Settings

I've never belonged at any table,
but I pass
the salt and looked up

which fork to use
in an etiquette book.

All my family's dead so nobody's
left that knows there's an Indian
girl with a sick head
who grew up poor and sometimes
likes to fuck women gone
and snuck into this little fête.
They don't look too close

because I got no color
and haven't been homeless
in years. Taught myself how to talk
right with sitcoms—these days,
I only slip up sometimes. Usually
when the drinks kick in or in catching

the smell of a fellow interloper,
overlooked uninvited guest. And we smile,
tight lips coating teeth because a feast
is always better when it's free

and a gorging
always sweeter for the starved.

Rezervations

I didn't grow up on the reservation—my Indian
summers were literal. The hot months gasped me in,
all pudgy pale legs and feet like my mom's. My reservations
were in hushed English while the elders slipped through Cherokee,
sounding cool as hose water on worn yellow plastic. My name
was over-seasoned between warm brown lips, their eyes
crinkling with flavors of *doesn't belong*s and a dusting
of cruelty. Some relative I've forgotten
would translate at times, between snaps at the charred cob
and rheumy butter down the chin. They told me

I was reserved, too quiet, too white, and I left
my shoes on indoors. My first cycle rushed like a plague
the summer I turned twelve, a slaughtering, a whole
new Trail. I didn't tell anyone, shoved napkins
down my shorts, held my breath
through the rocky waves. My redness

is on the inside, something too precious
or filthy to let shine in the fiery Oklahoma sun. Now,

I make reservations in restaurants bursting
with pretenses, where deer
heart tartare is presented with boredom, a quivering
quail egg riding naked on horseback. Bison burgers are stacked high
with foraged berry glacé and we call the fry bread
doughnuts, smother them with bacon or bright cereal
to go with the side of irony. I was never

one of them. But I pretend,
and I plait my hair, and I know my tribal
enrollment by heart. It's reserved permanent
into my hippocampus, real as Mom's high
arches, lingering as rusty stains on
underwear that chewed into slabs of thighs
struggling doggedly at the tired seams.

You Look Something

My best pieces, my showstoppers
are the ones they can't quite grasp.
You look something—that's what they say
when my cheekbones don't match
my whiteness, or my eyes
just aren't quite right. And I'm not
offended—far from it—I'm grateful,
immensely pleased
to be as solid as *Something*.

What's the other hand
I could have drawn? To look
Nothing, not worth a closer inspection,
as godawful *Same* as them? Of course,
they never guess right.

Latina, especially Mexican,
that's their favorite. Because when you look
Something along the West Coast corridor
you must have struggled your way up
from Mexico. Your blood must
have been muddled in California,
skin blanched as you rooted
up north. But sometimes,
sometimes,
they stumble in the right direction.

Like the old man who waited
till you left, turned whip fast and asked,
Are you Native? And I reveled in getting caught,
in being seen. But before I could answer,
before he could grapple his prize,
I love Indian women flew from his lips
like spittle, an airborne fetish. Still,
I bought his car, I touched his hand,
and I played the part he wanted—
the quiet Indian girl
who looked something.

What the Body Remembers

I was trained to look at the chest when jabbing
and hooking to the face. It does more
than keep the chin down. It dehumanizes
the target—that's more important than reading
the fear or strategies in their eyes. There were times
I felt a vomer bone give beneath my fist, sucked
flecks of spittle that wasn't my own spraying like perfume
across my lips and yet
I never saw their face. The fighting days
are over, but the body never forgets. My knuckles
are woven with burst veins like cracked glass. I still breathe
with a rush through the teeth when I carry
heavy loads. And when I pass someone on the street
whose eyes crawl over me like hungry spiders,
my eyes still shoot to their chest, nestling
my chin like a newborn into the fold and tensing
my stomach, my spirit, for the hit.

A Catholic Funeral

Let loose the noose, Rosalind,
kick off the kitchen chair. Hang yourself
like a lady, your father's good tie
wrapped 'round your neck.
Don't you remember,
you promised, *we* promised
to stay? Why else ask your brother
to teach us to fight, pick out the fat
fake gems from our rings? Free the metal
claws to rake up her face, make
the *Whores* and *Sluts* stop sailing
down the halls to pinch our butts
and skirt our thighs. Do you know
(you'd love this), at your funeral
the priest said you were in hell?
Pray for her soul. You'd have squeal-
laughed like always, asked if the fried
chicken was free. Your mother kept
a closed casket—I don't know
why. Aren't dead girls pretty, don't they
wear those marks like prize hickies? I wanted
to see you, came to see you. Barreled down the night
interstate with my cheap black dress
hanging like a ghost in the back seat,
poking at my shoulder and holding steady
like a sticky, scared shadow in my blind spot.

An Event Worth Celebrating

Run hard (like you mean it)
from a life that's uneventful,
for it's events that make a life.
My mother taught me the product
of being afraid. Of staying inside,
of what happens when agoraphobia
snaps you up like wanting pelicans.
It's quite possible

my life is already half over. Is over.
Could end today or maybe
I'll outlast them all. Each event
folds me over (I'm cake mix
with surprise flour balls and grainy
sugar goodness heading happy
to the blender). Every event
adds another buttercream rose

to my icing, an extra pinch
of salt to my insides. Who cares
how hot the oven gets? How many
hungry mouths wait, milk
cups in hand, on the other side?

Stack me layer-layer high, add
the sprinkles and fondant pieces.
I'm an event that demands celebration,
a party they'll talk about (especially
when the drinks kick in)
for *years* past my sell-by date.

Birthdays

The morning I turned thirty-five,
I asked the women orbiting my life
to meet me in the forest at dawn. It meant
getting up at four-thirty, being the first
car on the glittering asphalt, boyfriends
and lovers who wouldn't understand. Slipping
out before toddlers unclenched
their dream fists. Which of you would come

after all these years? It was stupid,
it was childish, all *Prove that you care*s
and *Show me you love me*s. I know that,
but I wanted, I needed, I was desperate
to see who would be there

before the birds, in the hours when rabbits
felt safe over human footprints. And it was nobody

I would have imagined, the quietest of sisters
who came, walked beside me, shot
fast as homemade bottle rockets
through the darkest morning hours.

Childhood

Two memories from when I was three
define my mother and father. A bath in the chipped
tub bubbling from generous squirts of dish
soap that dried my skin. We could never
afford the real things.
The plastic reptile squirt gun, half
full. My father came in
to shave his neck, swiping the blade neatly
around his moustache. When he finished,
he turned and scanned my naked body.
I shot him in the face,
scrubbed away his searching eyes and that
is how I learned what a gun is for.

I suckled my mother's breast until I could speak
because she wanted me to. The warm milk
filled my mouth, spreading to my limbs
like a drug. I lay on her chest in their bed,
a cartoon boxing match between a chicken
and a lamb on the TV. They squealed in one ear,
her heart beat in the other. As a bell rang and the animals
began circling, the nipple engorged
against my tongue, grotesque and huge, and that
is when I learned what teeth are for.

Years later, I watched my best friend's
five-year-old daughter
try to cover her mother's
chest with a blanket while her infant brother
was breastfed. A child discovers shame
as quickly as a farm animal
gets the metal bolt to the brain.

Disarming

My psychologist says (don't you love
when poets start like this?)
she suspects
I've been neutralizing my brain
for years. You see,
this particular organ has a way
of fucking up time and space.
More than we'd like to think,
it doesn't store trauma right—
lets it stick in the hippocampus
when in actuality that shit
should have gone prefrontal cortex
deep years ago. Stress, after all,
feeds psychosis. *That,* she said,
is why you need to write. I've been self-
medicating without the meds
my whole life. *What luck*
(can you believe it?)
that all my drugs are free.

Lattes and Labiaplasty

How good are you at unpacking? Real
damn good and fast—I beat everyone
at emptying the suitcase after vacation.
No, I mean your feelings, your emotions. Oh, real
fucking good. I slam those things into drawers
and closets so quick you can't be certain,
not totally, that was a stain you saw
on the sleeve. All these new words
are so careful, the phrases so contrived. Nobody
wants to be all woman, and here I am
apologizing for not envying his cock
or whipping out credit cards
for labiaplasty. On the inside,
I picture a half-man goat sucking
a flute when I say I'm pansexual,
such a ridiculous word for lust
without limits. Who cares
whom I bed or what my testosterone
levels are today? Unpack this, dismantle
that, something about patriarchy,
and pretend women have zero privileges.
How's this for privilege: I pass
as white and all the freedom
that carries, will never be falsely
accused of rape, and when I wear high heels
I trade perceived weakness for doors held
open and comped lattes with foam
like waning orgasms. We set the price,
finger the terms, and choose by the day
the space we spoon from this world.

An Anorexia Thing

It's an anorexia thing—we watch
our hair fall like drunks, tangled between bony
fingers in the shower while the down
on our arms, face, chest flourish
in a sad attempt to keep us warm. We shake
like old women in apartments others call *roasting*
as they slip off their jackets so we can judge
the fat of their arms, slabs of flesh jiggling
fresh as meat on hooks. The thing
about anorexia is we love our bodies

like an abusive boyfriend loves his woman,
an alcoholic loves the bottle, as
a junkie loves the next taste. How thin
can I get before the bones break
through the skin? How much less
can I weigh before I float down the streets,
a ghost to the masses but an angel
to few? We don't talk
about it, but I recognize my own,

and it's staggering in the war zone.

What the Lord God Planted

I named her Eden and saved her
(or maybe that was someone else). She
was seventeen, got here tucked
into a quick buck maker's overcoat (this
was before the planes went down).
We drove for miles, my college
roommates and I, down a gravel drive
and into a place where a greenhouse
dwarfed a ranch-style. Eden slipped away
minutes before I came, gliding over bubble
gum and leaving a trail of mess like Taylor's
Agnes—I loved her immediately. Demolition
crews had found her balled up in dirty walls
after her smuggler fled the crumbling apartments,
and for five years she was mine. Did you know
many snakes are like pit bulls—they don't strike
in succession? Their fangs snap out from the fold,
jaws lock tight as pickle jars. She bit me once,
an accident,
needle points piercing cagina. I did nothing,
held still, saw the sharp brown eyes push down
the fog and waited
while she worked her mistake from my flesh.

"Passing"

I was twelve before I realized my father wasn't white.
Until then I thought nothing
of his clay-colored skin, eyes dripping
like honey, or ropes of black licorice hair
snaking alive and furious down his back.
My breasts sprang early, hips splayed
wide as an overeager invitation
with bones pushing unforgiving
against my own skin, pale and quiet
as the illness. You took me to Radio Shack,
your syrupy southern drawl wrapping like a shy gift
around the simple words,
My wife put something on hold,
and the young clerk, not a decade older than me,
looked at both of us with blatant disgust,
loathing, and a shot of envy
even I could sniff out, like a dog
or a wild thing.

Is this your wife? he asked, and my chest
was in a painful awakening of an instant,
freakishly large, my hips
unable to slam shut, and you
too stunned to be ashamed or angered just whispered,
That's my daughter before walking out, the snakes gone still,
but for the years I'm too sorry to take back,
the years until the cancer sucked you dry,
I felt it for both of us,
felt it in my thighs built like a horse
and my lips too ripe for a child,
in every year after labor-heavy year
I refused to be seen with you, I'm so sorry
that I saw you gut punched and ugly as a man.

Red Delicious

You had a Red Delicious sticker plastered
to your foreman badge. As a child
I didn't know *Apple* was a bad word, the same
as *Oreo* or *Twinkie*. When I asked what it meant,
you just flashed those dazzling white teeth and said,
It's what they call us Indians. You owned it,
took pride in it. Reclaimed it. What was so wrong
about being something natural, something healthy
that produces those strong, thick ivories, something
delectable?
But not you. You, my father said,
You look just like your mother. God,
she was beautiful in her youth. All long, thick
hair flying behind the motorcycle like a wedding
dress train, starved down to ant-like
waist from meals of mustard and lettuce leaves.
But how I wanted your toasted skin—mine
was so pallid next to yours. I craved that delicious
red coloring and,

as a child,

soaked chestnut into my skin day after day,
roasting in my mother's tanning bed, letting the cancer
sink in slowly, a dirty marinade
that made me look like you. The ugliness
didn't show till decades later

and by then you were gone, smoke,
fragments of bone burned to ashes a lifeless
gray shade, boring, nothing like you,

and with not a trace of scarlet.

Nvda Diniyoli *(Children of the Sun)*

The scent of your moustache wax knocks
me back, an aroma of clove cigarettes
from my early twenties—the college years
when small murders of us flocked to fire
escapes in the crumbling buildings of the urban
campus. Even then I knew I didn't belong, the first
on my mother's side to go to college,
the first in my father's generation
to speak English with not a whisper
of Cherokee, though he'd forgotten
all but the easies—*usdi*: small,
alasgisda: dance, *ale ayv galieliga*:
I am happy. They beat the language out
in Indian boarding schools alongside other bad habits
like lying and pride. I snuck into this life quietly,
a cat burglar, my white face tattooed
permanent into my skin, an imposter
among the golden girls and boys.
My secret I held close where all the lies
are kept, under baggy shirts and tucked
into bras, pressed close as lovers
against my speeding heart. Years later,
finding you,
it felt like coming home—the hint of cloves,
moustache like my father,
skin brown-sugared as cut chai, and Us, glorious
Nvda Diniyoli: Children
of the Sun.

Recipe for Moong Daal

Look at me like you did
the first time you made me moong daal,
my Otis Redding and Eartha Kitt
uncertain in the tiny, dirty kitchen
and you, oiled black ringlets
falling like madmen on your brow.
Press me hard against the counter,
knead your hands
into my waist, trace your fingers
over hip bones,
invade my mouth with yours
between the squealing whistles
of the pressure cooker.
Oil heating in the saucepan, dusted
with cumin seeds,
watch them struggle till they're the same
soft brown as your hairless arms
pulling me close, between the stove
and you. Tear dried red
chilies into the pan, adding the spice.
Dice slick green peppers
on a makeshift cutting board, thick
fingers deftly working the small,
fragile slivers with the same certainty
they handle me. Grate in ginger root
with rhythmic practice, add the curry leaves.
Onions and turmeric are next
as I lean against the refrigerator,
breathing you in, the scent of your sweat
with the bite of red onions.
Grab me tight, taste my neck
while the turmeric spreads golden
in the hiss. A pinch of asafoetida,
all the pan holds poured into the cooker,
and for ten minutes you deconstruct
me, long ginger-scented fingers
stained yellow brushing my lips,
black onion-teary eyes searching
and the blues
crying like forgotten children.

Alpha to Omega

You get cookies at the Gujarati temples, proof
that you were *good*. That you showed up. That you whispered
the right prayers to the right idols. (Of course,
I didn't know the prayers. I followed you like a puppy,
quiet and obedient). Here's what I learned: It takes
the exact same time for you to say the prayers
as it does me to recite
the Greek alphabet in my head (a hangover
from the college years). *Alpha*, tap the turmeric
blend on the forehead. *Beta*—the same word
your mother calls me (daughter). *Gamma*,
wonder why I had to cover my hair
when all these other women didn't.
Delta and *Why aren't these people looking
at me? Am I not so different? Epsilon*,
these are the smells of your childhood,
the sounds of your memories. All the way
to *Omega*, the end and the sweets.
I've always loved desserts, the rewards
that close those firsts and leave a slick
of guilt on your tongue, crumbled
evidence of goodness on lips.

Ingredients of Love

If food is love, what does it mean
for those who starve ourselves? *Eat this*,
says Maa, gajar halwa she shredded
all morning till her fingers burned orange.
I'm full, I say, pushing
her love off my plate, feeding
her sacrifice to the bin, to the birds,
to the raccoons that forage
at dusk. *Taste this*, you tell me,
fingers pinching palak paneer
gone limp. *I'm fasting*, I tell you,
scooting the bowl of our vows
back into your space. Over and over,
year following year, the love
is ladled and forked, plated
and whisked again and again
toward my clamped-shut mouth.
Maybe tomorrow, I keep saying,
the words by now stale
and crumbling out, an explosion
of yesterday's confections.

My Body, My Self

I've put you through so much, and still
you hold me up—shaky
legs and bumpy arms. The years I fed you scraps
at best, you lapped up every crumb, used
each speck to carry on. The times
I beat you stupid, beyond
the ability to stand, flinch from the traumas
or keep fists above breastbone. Remember
the time I slipped you the ecstasy, only
it was some kind of speed-meth monster
that left us lurching in the Atlanta heat? Me,

I would have left me by now. *Long* ago.
But you,

you've stayed, solid. Through the disrespect,
the slaps, the ridicule and pummeling
abuses. And not once did you break. Give up
for good. Didn't gather all your everythings,
but stood tall on too long legs
and screamed, demanding for more.

Look at All the Beautiful

Kept private like our genitals
are supposed to be,
you'll find the good
trails. The ones nobody
talks about, where blackberry brambles
shoot through old bark chips
like zombie hands and spiders weave
wet threads licking your face
come dawn. It's not easy,

keeping quiet. Cradling secrets.
Like children,
they get loud and heavy. They squirm
and you want to drop them, see
their little heads explode like watermelons.

I wanted to show you,
look—

how the trail spreads her legs
like un unabashed woman. Choose
your fork and trust. Look
how the creeks and rivers bore
their own way, not giving a damn
for the carnage. See me
here, grinding through the morning
light. And once more, look, just look.

Look at all the beautiful.

Land Lords

We pay rent to the animals,
to the raccoons who plunder the plum
trees, smacking and swallowing
like little hunchbacked beasts. To the squirrels
who pick the most pregnant of apples
and leave pine cone trails
on the patio. To Oregon's giant house
spiders, scrabbling frenzies across oak floors,
whisked out with Windex-soaked newspapers
to keep on willing a mate outdoors. The skunks
with their cactus tails and viper heads,
nosing through spilled cereal
from our mornings on the oiled swing.
And the deer, whose clumsy steps
betray their graceful thighs, calves
like fine buffet legs and breasts riding proud.
For them we pay in fat blackberries,
splitting cherries and red pears. But the roses …

the roses …

those I dust in curry powder
and tight pinches of turmeric. Perennials
are for us, and the animals, the poor things,
they blanch and choke at the bite.

Recipe for an Indian

How much Indian are you? All of it,
red velvet proofs deep in my folds.
Fry bread thighs undercooked, whipped
merengue cheekbone peaks,
and a blackened cut of feather
tattoo marinating over childhood
scars, biopsy stitches, and mole seasonings
from a life of willing the sweetness
burning inside to rise, rise, rise.

Bad Indian

Bad Indian, not a speaker—who gives
a damn if they beat it out of my father
in residential boarding school? They say
"Pretendian" & an old man with creamed
blue eyes cackled after demanding my ancestry,

"Everyone's a Cherokee." I apologize

for green eyes, pale skin. It's not enough
to soften cries of "Wana'be clan!
Elizabeth Warren all over
again." Once an elder
vet spit on my wanting
cheekbones, my braids, that I didn't know
Lakota. I did not choose my skin

or the trauma curdling rancid
through my blood. We are born into creation
disasters, settled war zones, armed
with chanced defenses, so forgive me

that ivory is my weapon. Poachers try
& they show teeth, dressed
in polyester & crafted altruism,
but I am fast & I remember. I'm *kamama*—you really
think you got us all? We still roam
our land; thirteen thousand years is a single heart
beat in the whole story. I am telling you, listen:

I am hungry, matriarch
made too young. My grief's too big
to contain & like Damini I will starve
24 days to die from broken
chambers—and by god, how you will keen,
spill cracked-bone to your knees, pay
homage to my skeleton, to this bad Indian.

On the Runway

Tell me I'm svelte, tell me I'm thin,
that my walk is defectless, limb after limb,
that my cheekbones are just the right
daggering peaks, not too Cherokee, just barely
a shadowed half-breed, that my shoulders roll back
quite effortlessly,
yet not from a decade of Camels
and Wheel, but a bend born
of nature, genetic lotteries, still
that my chest rises grandly as foam on the tide,
my starvation was worth it,
this swaggering stride.

Writing

I always say this is the last one, but that's
when I'm empty. When I just got it good—
it's easy then. To act like I've had my fill,
like the craving won't come again, like
I won't say *Okay* just once more, spill
my insides all over. Weave my fingers
through the guts and intestines, spread
out my all for the world to pick apart.

A Consenting Platypus

The septuagenarian served me tea
in the garden of her thatched roof
British cottage. Between spoons
of fish pie and too much Prosecco,
I told her about the best-selling erotica
I ghostwrite. How people don't like sex
until at least chapter nineteen.
She asked me about bestiality, which of us
animals are the nastiest. *No, incest
and animals are my hard lines*.
"That's too bad," she demurred. "It's incredible
what one can do
with a consenting platypus."

Pulitzer Prize Pig

Pulitzer Prize Pig spoke of what it means
to be ***** as a ***** man with a look
the look *that* look
women were born knowing
how to read. I knew
that look   *the* look
at fifteen when the AP teacher crouched
beside my desk in the dark
while flashes of syphilis
and gonorrhea shuddered
across the projector screen. (Still, even now,
I hear the tired clicking of the tapes.)
I knew the look,   saw *a* look
at eleven when grown men whistled
at my unfolding hips and high
school boys rolled Corollas
along middle school parking lots
with eyes that spider-scurried
pressed breasts. And I knew, I saw
that look,   *his* look
at three. In the bathtub, I learned shame—
I shot my father
in the eye with a plastic alligator squirt
gun and never bathed with open doors again.
Pulitzer Prize Pig sidled up close, nosed for nipple
drinkers and sniffed out my slop. Trough walls
are low but sticky, slick beside sties,
and boars are happy with scraps.

Recollections of the Training Days

Dogs with prong collars adjust to the pinch—
that was me, immune to the warm blood trickles
when he petted my car's hood
to see if I'd strayed that day. My skin grew tough
against the spikes, so I got used

to The Next telling me I was *almost thin*
and should only speak
when commanded—like a dog,
like a bitch, like something that scurries
on all fours tonguing up compliments
alongside filthy water bowls.
And then there was you. There are times
you make me feel like an animal

in the right ways. Times
when I need to re-learn tricks I lost
over the years like chewed
up toys or buried, cherished things.
I remember the choking nails in the deepest

and darkest of nights and how it felt
when you slipped them off, easily
and quickly
like my threadbare shirts
when you undress me in the mornings.

The Penthouse in the Pearl

We folded some lovely
times into that year, pinches
of memories with just the right
amount of bite. Like the time you asked
what my best sad song was
and we danced like drunks
on your balcony, aches and stretches
above the city. The night I told you
to kiss me like a teenager
and for once you did. The evening
I stole away from my party when you called
and I demanded you buy me contact
lens solution—though you swore
you could make it yourself. That morning
you told me you loved me and I breathed
deep and steady, faking sleep. I didn't want
to ruin the simplicity of what we'd done
or slip into someone else's life
like a shiny robe left forgotten
and swaying on the bathroom hook.

The Temporary Nature of Being

Bedded down in the woods,
the houses rest on stilts, dangerous,
dangling like sleeping children
on top bunks. We tiptoe like gluttons
across the Cascadia faults, as if
the sweets stuffed in cupboards
and ice cream cradled in freezers are fair
trade for our lives. The experts call us
woefully unprepared as we bow tangled
heads over sugary cereal, the morning
news unable to shock. Tsunamis overseas,
floods on the East Coast—we're so sure
nothing can touch us here, not in the Wild
West, never where gold rushes raged
or martinis were brought to life. Forest hugs
me close, the occasional sharp thorny fingernails
tracing taut calves or hoggish spider webs
licking my face. One day,
soon,
it will all come crashing down: The West
Hills homes indie bands made famous,
the teetering decks like behemoths,
dumb and feeble scarecrows in the sky.

~~mURDERED & mISSING iNDIGENOUS wOMEN~~*

A girl gotta grow up, leave the rez, & do we talk about it? Igido called twice for bail but both were after a Tahlequah fall, & high with opioid they drove right through a gate. Bolted up the highway—bare feet & all—hitched a ride via lifted truck to take her far away before 911 with, *The devil up & took the car.* Dad left right outta jail, headed to the Pacific, & gave away that plot of Cherokee a year later. *You'da hated it* & I probably would have.

No folks gonna talk of them gone ones anymore. They look at me all, *Got some bless'n on y'all*—after all, no cop has got me (yet). No reason, really. Everyone else, the hole fam'ly, gone & sear to memory the creak of a cell's cot frame long ago. None of y'all can fathom at the places gonna call for me. They gone & settle prefrontal cortex, & that seems an okay place to some.

At 15, we 3 bunked all day 4 an aged wee-jee game: We'd all be dead by 23, and we laughed and made a bet 4 the chance. An ATV ate Ann at 18 and then a fancy cable hung by Althea came next. Hadn't even nudged me 4 that plan. And when death happen that way, we can't talk any decent way.

No one talk anythin' of funeral 1 or 2 & I kept lookout for a face I knew while the Catholic father went on & on about killin' another or you & prayin' for both. Father, what type of Native turn Catholic, anyway? Who tuck that in their brain? All thru junior year, neither talk of church or nothin'. Creator not have way to fix it, then?

Who up and say so long to that god? Why do NDNs stand for that nat'l song? So many of us wash away, walk away, drag and drug away, and nobody's com'n back from that havoc of war.

Some of us hate a couple, "wo," tacked to the 1st of what we call big boys. But with Tsaligi it's fixed—Asgaya, male. Agehya, female. Why make that "M" all a mess, wave wide those legs & smile? It's the 1st of the alphabet, debut of music, the call all of us made as we slipped to this place. & maybe that's the space us Agehya go to. The alpha, the basis, the middle of this wasted home.

I ran away, still a kid, and my mama said *why why why* until pills kick'd in. With my dad and sis, *Luv y'all* was last. With my mama, I try and say I try. I try. I try.

When they ask where we went, where we go, why gone permanent cloys & flanks so close, why holes & channels swallow w/ ease & no one asks or even seems to say that's strange, remember. Remember: those who are gone never go that far. We are here. We stay. To be forgotten means an agreement's complete—that's not ever gonna happen

&

Untitled

For those who say I should write of Sherman Alexie's
alleged sexual misconduct and not of Junot Diaz's:
hush. Eat what's on your plate or move
to another table. To those who say I shouldn't talk
of Indian-ness because I'm *just half*,
shut up. When you're old, you'll know
the knowing of insides
with unmatched casing. (And you'd milk
thick privilege from colostrum
to dryness, too). For those who say
catcalls and harassment are the same
(#metoo) as rape (*We're all in
this together!*), fuck off and fall
crack-boned knee thankful
you *can only imagine*
the feeling of strange fingers
probing your cervix in familiar halls
while the doorman sleeps. Just as I
don't know the fall-apart of rape. For you
who says it's no surprise,
my mother's death, ask, *Is it a good
thing or bad thing she's gone?* Quiet (like her)—
we don't question the dead,
for their tongues are defenseless,
amongst the first to go in the retort.

My Mother('s) Remains

Do you want to go to the Bahamas? I opened
my mother's ashes and was taken
by the color. Somehow, I thought she'd be slate,
but she was like Florida,

coarse and tawny. What remains
is heavier than you'd think, full
of bones and grit. The weight
tugs you down. As I spooned
her into the little glass
jar, I remembered being six,

my aunt packed tight
in a carboard urn while the lot
of us boarded a shaky propeller
plane. The pilot never said
to hold it low, let the wind
lap what's left—she swarmed
us like wild things, left a thick
coating, and we licked her chars
from philtra. Brackish and dry, she shot
to our innards, became a burrowing,

permanent part of us all. I thought,

I don't want my mother
to stay. Haunt my organs,
blow like smoke through dreams. How long
can someone stick
to the familiar? Cling scared
to all we hate? Like the gold
beggar children in Mexico, I brushed
her from my skirt and held my breath
against her dust. Maybe,
if I sprinkle her in the turquoise
of the tropics, salt the rim
a little more, she'll finally
(after so, so many years) release
those bitten nails and let me go.

Beebe Farms: Closed August, 2017

The orchard went last
summer. At the time
I didn't know the end
was nipping feral
at my ankles. Death makes us
want to fill our bellies, drown
the flashbacks. That's why
we reach for fucks we won't
remember and pray for pregnancies
swollen with regrets. When she died,
nostalgia skipped clean
over me straight into the trash.
I wanted nothing, no blouses
to sniff, old trophies to dust or scraps
of handwriting already burned
brand-hot into cortex.
All I wanted
was to leave the dying trees
behind and forget childhood
desire paths overgrown. Brambles
spread like disease on familiar
acres and the brittle limbs
shot upward in prayer—but not once
did I drive by the pastures
or look skyward with cold faith
for anything close to a signal.

A Priest and an Indian Walk Into a Bar

The priest cooked me risotto
while I tongued olives and dry wine.
Barefoot and drunk, we compared
best sad operas and stumbled
through yoga poses in the gloaming. After,
giggling like schoolchildren through the buzz,
sidling up to a bar bellowing for bourbon
and crushed ice. *Fill it all the way up!*
We danced to ABBA and my skirt
fell down, but I never once thought
to confess more than was settled
or ask anything close to forgiveness.

The Lecture

You think I want to be here?
Listen, I was young like you once, too. I thought
of traveling the world, and I did a little, and let me tell you

there's nothing romantic about drunken Korean men
vomiting on your shoes in the subway or Ticos on the beaches
holding your hand and sucking down iced sodas poured in plastic bags
while they give thirteen-year-old local girls the up-down.

Just listen to me: I wanted to go to Iowa. I stood
on the murderous barstools at the Yamhill Pub on open mic night
and told roomfuls of belligerent strangers about my one-night stands.
I read *The Bell Jar* and fancied myself Esther
or thought, you know, if I'd just been born in the right decade
they'd have called me more handsome than Marlon Brando,
and I could've been high every night

or crafted the perfect suicide letter. Listen,
I've done all that and let me tell you something you already know,

that thing that keeps tapping at your brain when you wake up at four
in the morning, it's already started
to slip away and you better pray,
you better pray,
you at least had the foresight during one of those too-late nights
when you were wrapping your legs around someone whose face
you don't remember or whose face is just too ridiculously
familiar now that you at least did something—

something—
to make damn sure there's *something* waiting for you on the other end
because if there's not, if you didn't think you'd get old too
like all the rest of us, that's not going to stop
the freight train that's barreling straight for you,

and it's going to smash the living hell out of everything because it can,
because it doesn't care, because that's it's nature, it's the scorpion
riding horseback here and just like you, it will roll right over
something, someone, at some time considered precious
and barely even wonder what that bump was
as it keeps screaming into the night.

To Grin Macabre

Some are scared of the starved, others
arch away in awe, afraid what we have
will catch. A few hover close, fruit flies thirsty
to lick up tips—hopeful
to become one of us. When your scaffolding
begins to show, it's not all at once.
First the bottom rung of ribs
peek out like a shy debutante. Next,
maybe your cheekbones protrude
a little more than they should, a sudden
pergola riding where baby fat cheeks
used to pudge (where the apples
once blossomed). Hold out your hands—
press your fingers together tight.
Can you see the rays? Skinny enough
and it bursts like heaven between the bars, only
your knuckles can touch. Beautiful, right?

But here's what they don't tell you: People
start falling away as easily
as your hair down the drain. Nobody knows
how to talk to a skeleton. All bones, it's hard
to work your tongue. Hold on
to friendships. Make love
when your stomach's raging in the empty.
So let us go,
let me burrow deep into the earth
where I belong and the others like me
turn in their graves, disturb their plots
to grin macabre at the newcomer.

The Photograph

When I asked to see a photo of your parents,
it was to gauge my enemy, the people
who had a neat row of women lined up
for you in Mumbai, who would turn
you away if they ever knew the color
of my skin or my American name. I wanted
to see you in them, a shadow
of your brimming-over lips,
if your mother's eyes were opaque
ink like yours, if your father's cruelty
was palpable through the film. What you showed me
was an aging couple, shoulders
hugging in like damp wings. Your mother
was blowing out her birthday candles
and there was nothing of you in them.

How to Oil an Indian Man's Hair

Your apartment smells like coconut oil
in the mornings. Watch the Vatika bottle
spin lazy circles in the microwave to be sure
it doesn't melt. You sit between my legs,
your dry naked feet crossed and me
perched like a fragile, cautious bird
on the buttery leather couch. Pull over the cheap
dark square table, fold a paper napkin twice,
pour the milky warm oil into my palm,
place the bottle on the napkin.
I wear nothing but your boxer shorts,
your low *tsk tsk* as the oil slips
through my thin fingers, burrows between bones,
falls onto pallid thighs white as flashes
against your skin. Begin at your scalp,
rub it in.

Add more oil, finger comb your long black hair,
curling, waking snakes unwinding down your back.
Take off your glasses, thumb your temples. I'm greased
as a dirty dog to my elbows. Stop, wait,
Still

for your giant perfect hands
(puppy hands, my janu)
to swallow mine easily as a cobra. You
smelled like coconuts

cracked open, the sweetness
released, fled. Wild.

Let Me Go Quietly

I don't want anyone saying they knew me
should I die ahead of others or when I'm gone
before the whispers. I don't want women
I can't stand, who despise me pound for pound,
muttering niceties over raw earth or prettying up
memories alongside casseroles. I don't want
men sniffing around, saying how lovely
I was when they used to comment on my bones,
the propensity of my skin to mar. I want you

to be the only one to say my name like it mattered.
The body of my pieces I wrote for you, the meat
of my words thickened from our story and the heat
from what we bore isn't for the gawkers
or forced, awkward acquaintances. Let them forget me,
feel satisfied that their bodies wore out last,
store up those social graces like pinching shoes
they'll never wear. You're the witness
to my entirety, attestant of my every,
the only I want following
my loping footsteps into the deep.

"Eating Like a Bird, it's Really a Falsity"
—Norman Bates

You don't just decide to start eating again. It happens slow,
a groggy crawl and stumble out of a dream.
I didn't choose to starve myself.
I didn't choose to stop. It was a cycle, my own metamorphosis
full of Kafka leanings and sopping new wings.

Built up like an orgasm, I can't tell you
the foreplay, the spots touched that got me there,
the details of the teasing
or the fetishes reveled in (that's sacred),
but I can tell you this—I woke up
in Washington Park, stomping the trails behind the zoo.
Maybe it was the humbling houses of the West Hills,
or the reservoirs spreading like spilt champagne
at my feet, but on that day

I woke with a start. Past the rose test garden poached
with pale tourists, past the fountain where droplets sounded like
    church bells,
I climbed to the playground at the top of the hill,
slipped onto a swing and learned
all over again
how easy it is to fly. My god, it's a lovely thing
to face your fragility and still take flight. But birds,
"birds really eat a tremendous lot," so give me the fat ones
the thick ones, the ones burrowed down deep,
fill me with their earthiness until I choke from the grit,
desperate for air, neck arching and jaw flexing,
bones slight and delicate as a song.

Recovery

Recover is a funny word, like
what's buried that needs covering
again? What are we hiding in the dirt,
and will the worms crawl through
my fingers, roots tear
at my cuticles or bugs catch
in my nails? We cover up a lot—
our thighs the size of calves,
the hip bone sawing into thin flesh
stretched taught as tanning
hides. Let's dig it up once more,
spread it out under fluorescent
lights and delight in the ugly of it all.

How to Talk to the Dying

I looked up *What to say*
to the dying because words
get stuck in my hands. There's no good
answers. You died the same

way our father did, yellow
skin and lion eyes. What do you say

to your sister out

on the reservation? *I love you,*
that's it. Your husband told me

you smiled and poured
your own *Love*
you back into me

all the way down
through the wires. The voice

deep, dark and foreign
like a stranger's always is.

Mourning Lights

My father visited me in a cramped
Atlanta hotel room five years
after he died. It was hours since
I took the ecstasy from a drag
queen's bra, long after I faltered
through the doors of a basement
club on the other side of the city. I couldn't recall
how I'd got there—let alone the miracle
of slurring the right address in a taxi. The dawn's
pink fingers were just reaching in, trailing
across my wailing head, clawing fierce
into bruised eye sockets. I knew him

by his force, the dramatic entrance, that sizzle
in the air. I was still coming down, but in his glory
he hovered like a poltergeist in the room, lighting
up those cheap nylon sheets and bad prints
bright as a firecracker. In a panic I stuck
my head under the threadbare covers, sure
the ghosts would lose interest, the demons
wonder at my own magic when my wan moon face
disappeared with a snap. Weeks later I found my comfort,
my two fingers of numbness, smooth and strong—my father
came to me as ball lightning, a phenomenon explained
by science and dismissed as nature's freak show. But I know,

in the deepest, secret chambers of my heart,
he gathered all his essence, all his power, all
his everything to fire up my world, and I—
I hid like a coward, a shaken toddler,
his crowning disappointment in the dark.

All the Ways

Know that

just because we're quiet
doesn't mean we aren't railing inside.
We ate herring in red coats and I told you
all the ways I'd kill myself, how
your lips were wilder than the moon.
It's a lie

that we're born alone, die alone.
We arrive

through slick thighs,
wet bellies, and maybe
we'll never see our mothers again. Maybe
she'll stick to us like burned
batter all our lonely lives. And we'll die

with all those lovers, gone
mothers, animals that licked our hurts
knotted like stowaways
in the most secret
desolate chambers of our hearts.
They escort us, shaking

straight into the luminous.

Mark's Tumor (When I Needed It Most)

"How quickly this life does go by." Tonight
I wrote the last letters
to my poetry students. It's always been hard,
dishing out compliments (unless I really,
really mean it). My mother died
halfway through the class, a term
dedicated to confession and yoking
sadness from fingertips. *Tell me
your best sad secret. Write the love
letter you never sent, the one that hissed
a papercut into your flagina so you took
it as an omen.* How do I rank choice
of line breaks and liberties
with pantoums while my mother burns
at 1,800 degrees? Tell the octogenarian
that his piece on alpaca butter is shit
or the Iowa dropout I should be the one
at his feet? You don't, but the dead

are furtive messengers. The banker
sent it privately, a poem he'd been too shy
or wise to workshop
into neat numbness. He likened
his tumor to a peach beyond burst,
skin sloughing off like summer tans—and us,
our ridiculous grasping
of it all when in the end, "How quickly,

how quickly this life does go by."

Something Beautiful

I wrote something beautiful for you, come
let me watch your face ebb while I work
your waves like the moon. Never
have you said anything more
than *I like it*, your accent adorning
the words like one of your good watches.
I don't need
any more validation than this—
the curl of your lips as you scan the nakedness
of my poetry like a piece
of lit paper over uncertain flame.

When to Stay

They say I don't know when to leave. I say
they don't know
when to stay. What good comes
after the bars shut down, past the window
of *these shoes could go all night*? Knowing
when to stay is what brought me to you.
Knowing how to stay shot us
through the affairs, the culture battles, the year
I ran away to another land with another man
and yet you played stowaway
in my organs. When you know
when to stay, how to close down
the party and watch the lights come on,

you see everything. The way the floors
are caked in syrup and the booths
are worn to threads. How the dancers
wear their stretch marks and the barbacks'
fingernails are chewed. We stayed through
the last song, the final bathroom checks,
when the last dish was scraped of tots
and plopped into the machine—through the ugly
and into the empty morning streets
where New and Hope trudge soft
and amble on bare feet into the next.

Acknowledgments

"Place Settings" first appeared in *The Pangolin Review*, September 2018.

"Rezervations" first appeared in *The Elephant Magazine*, Feb. 2017.

"You Look Something" first appeared in *Yellow Medicine Review*, Mar. 2016.

"A Catholic Funeral" first appeared in *FLARE: The Flagler Review*, March 2020.

"An Event Worth Celebrating" first appeared in *The Long Island Literary Journal*, October 2017.

"Childhood" first appeared in *The Cossack Review*, June 2013.

"Disarming" first appeared in *The Pangolin Review*, September 2018.

"Lattes and Labiaplasty" first appeared in *Pointed Circle*, May 2018.

"An Anorexia Thing" first appeared in *The Anti-Languorous Review*, July 2020.

"Passing" first appeared in *Off the Coast*, 2013.

"Red Delicious" first appeared in *The Elephant Magazine*, Feb. 2017.

"Nvada Diniyoli: Children of the Sun" first appeared in *The Elephant Magazine*, Feb. 2017.

"Recipe for Moong Daal" first appeared in *Menacing Hedge*, May 2012.

"Alpha to Omega" first appeared in *Howl*, June 2017.

"My Body, My Self" first appeared in *Rigorous*, February 2018.

"Look at All the Beautiful" first appeared in *Dying Dahlia Review*, Feb. 2017.

"Land Lords" first appeared in *Clumsy Quips*, September 2017.

"Recipe for an Indian" first appeared in the anthology edited by Grace Bauer. *Nasty Women Poets: An Unapologetic Anthology of Subversive Verse*. Sandpoint: Lost Horse, 2017.

"Bad Indian" first appeared in *Rising Phoenix Review*, July 2018.

"A Consenting Platypus" first appeared in *The Dead Mule School of Southern Literature*, April 2018.

"Pulitzer Prize Pig" first appeared in *Pennsylvania English*, December 2018.

"mURDERED & mISSING iNDIGENOUS wOMEN" first appeared in *HCE Review*, April 2019.

"Untitled" first appeared in the anthology edited by Helen Dryden. *Whatever I Feel Like I Wanna Do, Gosh!* Leeds Arts University, 2019.

"My Mother('s) Remains" first appeared in *Raven Chronicles*, June 2018.

"A Priest and an Indian Walk Into a Bar" first appeared in the anthology edited by Jenny Forrester. *Unchaste Anthology*: Volume 2. Unchaste Readers, 2017.

"The Lecture" first appeared in *Furnicular Magazine*, September 2018.

"To Grin Macabre" first appeared in *Allegory Ridge*, July 2017.

"The Photograph" first appeared in *Viral Cat*, Oct. 2012.

"How to Oil an Indian Man's Hair" first appeared in *Eclectica Magazine*, Apr. 2012.

"Eating Like a Bird, It's Really a Falsity" first appeared in *Massachusetts Review*, 2020.

"How to Talk to the Dying" first appeared in *Causeway Lit*, Apr. 2017.

"Mourning Lights" first appeared in *Hobo Camp Review*, October 2017.

"All the Ways" first appeared in the anthology edited by David Meischen. *Poetry of the American Southwest #3: Weaving the Terrain.* Dos Gatos Press: 2017.

"Mark's Tumor (When I Needed It Most)" first appeared in *Pom Pom*, June 2018.

"When to Stay" first appeared in *REaDLips Press*, July 2017.

Author

JC Mehta is an interdisciplinary artist, poet, author of several books, and citizen of the Cherokee Nation. Much of their work is informed by space, place, and ancestry. Mehta has served as part of the Airlie Press collective as an editor and has been awarded a number of art and research fellowships, including a First Peoples Fund fellowship and Eccles Centre Visiting fellowship at the British Library. Poetry-in-residency posts have taken Mehta to Crazy Horse Memorial, the Shakespeare Birthplace Trust in Britain, and Halcyon Arts Lab in Washington DC. Book awards include gold at the IPPY Awards, Book Excellence Awards, and Reader Views Literary Awards.

Nothing feels better than home

While we at Meadowlark Press love to travel, we also cherish our home time. We are nourished by our open prairies, our enormous skies, community, family, and friends. We are rooted in this land, and that is why Meadowlark Press publishes regional authors.

When you open one of our fiction books, you'll read delicious stories that are set in the Heartland. Settle in with a volume of poetry, and you'll remember just how much you love this place too—the landscape, its skies, the people.

Meadowlark Press publishes memoir, poetry, short stories, and novels. Read stories that began in the Heartland, that were written here. Add to your Meadowlark book collection today.

Specializing in Books by Authors from the Heartland Since 2014

www.birdypoetryprize.com

Meadowlark Press created The Birdy Poetry Prize to celebrate the voices of this era. Cash prize, publication, and 50 copies awarded annually.

Entries Accepted: September 1 to December 1.

Final Deadline for Entries: December 1, midnight.

Entry Fee: $25

All entries will be considered for standard Meadowlark Press publishing contract offers, as well.

Full-length poetry manuscripts (55 page minimum) will be considered. Poems may be previously published in journals and/or anthologies, but not in full-length, single-author volumes. All poets are eligible to enter, regardless of publishing history.

See www.meadowlark-books for complete submission guidelines.

www.ingramcontent.com/pod-product-compliance
Lightning Source LLC
Chambersburg PA
CBHW071320080526
44587CB00018B/3293